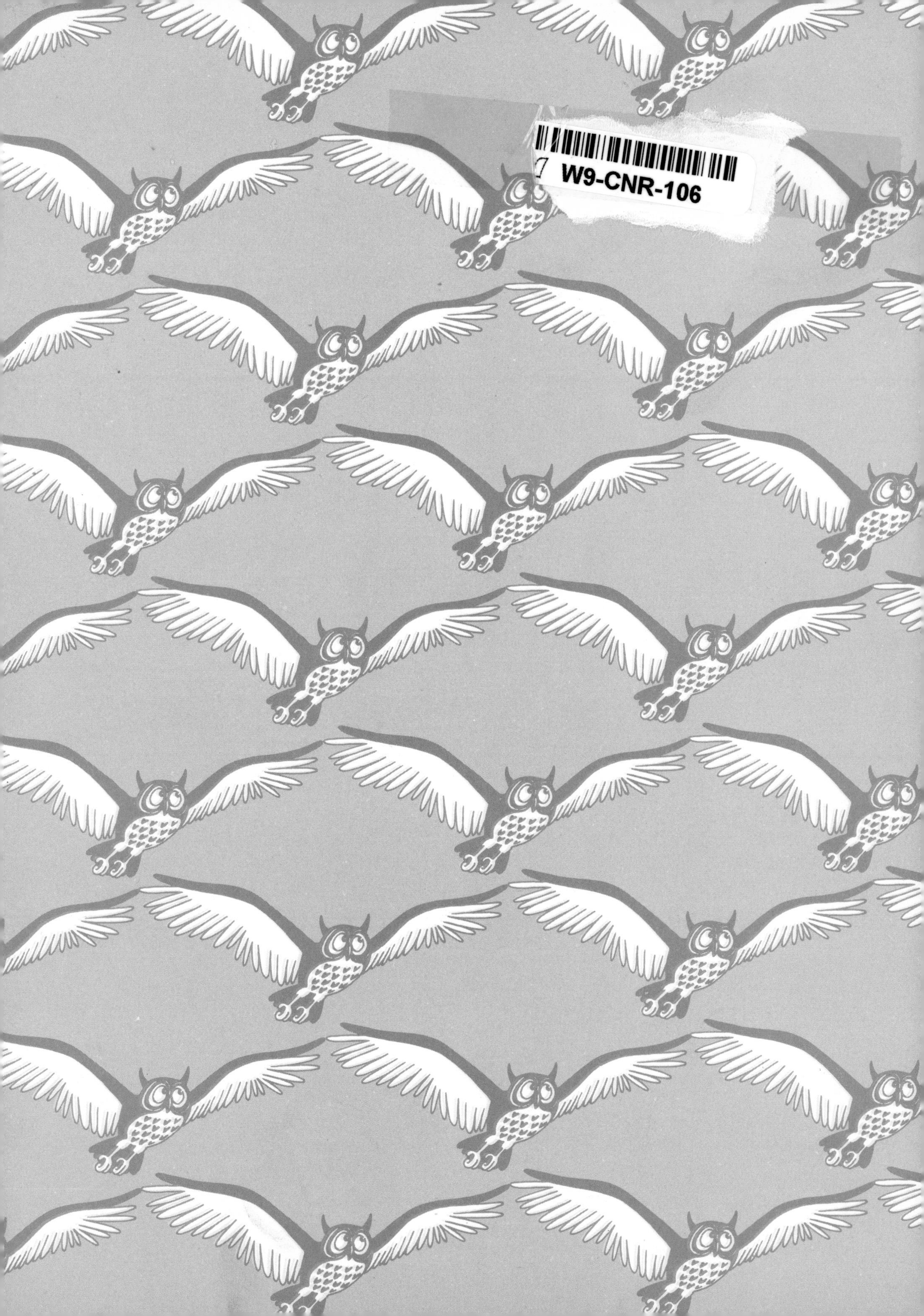

Answers to Questions Kids Ask ab

An OWL Magazine/Golden Press® Book

By the editors of OWL Magazine

ver Book #1

rds, Cats, Bats, UFOs and More

Edited by Katherine Farris
Art Direction by Nick Milton
Cover design by Elaine Groh

An OWL Magazine/Golden Press® Book

Printed in the U.S.A. by Western Publishing Company, Inc.
OWL Magazine is a trademark of The Young Naturalist Foundation.
GOLDEN®, GOLDEN® & DESIGN, and GOLDEN PRESS® are trademarks of Western Publishing Company, Inc.

Library of Congress Catalog Card Number 83-80459.
Canadian ISBN 0-919872-82-4
U.S. ISBN 0-307-12450-9

B C D E F G H I J

Published in Canada by Greey de Pencier Books, Toronto
Canadian Cataloguing in Publication Data
OWL's Question & Answer Book #1
(OWL Magazine/GOLDEN PRESS® Book)
Includes index.
ISBN 0-919872-82-4
1. Animals – Miscellanea – Juvenile literature.
2. Nature – Miscellanea – Juvenile literature.
I. Farris, Katherine. II. OWL (Toronto, Ont.).
QL49.A84 j570 C83-098046-6

What makes this book special?
Every year OWL, the Discovery Magazine for Children, is asked thousands of questions by readers. This book gives answers to those questions that have been asked most often. If you're interested in cats or bats, bugs or birds, sharks or UFOs, turn the page. Chances are you'll find lots of other things you always wanted to know about as well.

Why is a cat's tongue so rough?

A lick from a tabby is like being rubbed by sandpaper, but the flick of a tiger's tongue could tear your skin. All cats have comblike spikes called papillae on their tongues that they use for brushing their fur and scraping meat from bones. When they drink, the cat's papillae trap liquid on the tongue. The larger the cat, the larger and rougher the papillae.

Why do cats turn their ears around?

Cup your hands behind your ears and you'll understand better why cats can hear so well. But it's not only the funnel shape of a cat's ears that helps it to pick up sound. Every cat has up to 20 muscles in each ear so it can swivel them in almost any direction. Watch a cat do this while hunting. It's listening to every squeak and rustle, including some you can't hear at all.

Why does a cat's fur stand on end?

A cat's fur, consisting of large guard hairs and shorter underfur, protects its body from bites, scratches and hot and cold temperatures. Each guard hair is attached to a muscle that makes it stand on end whenever the cat is angry or alarmed. And because this is so startling to see, it is a very good scare tactic indeed.

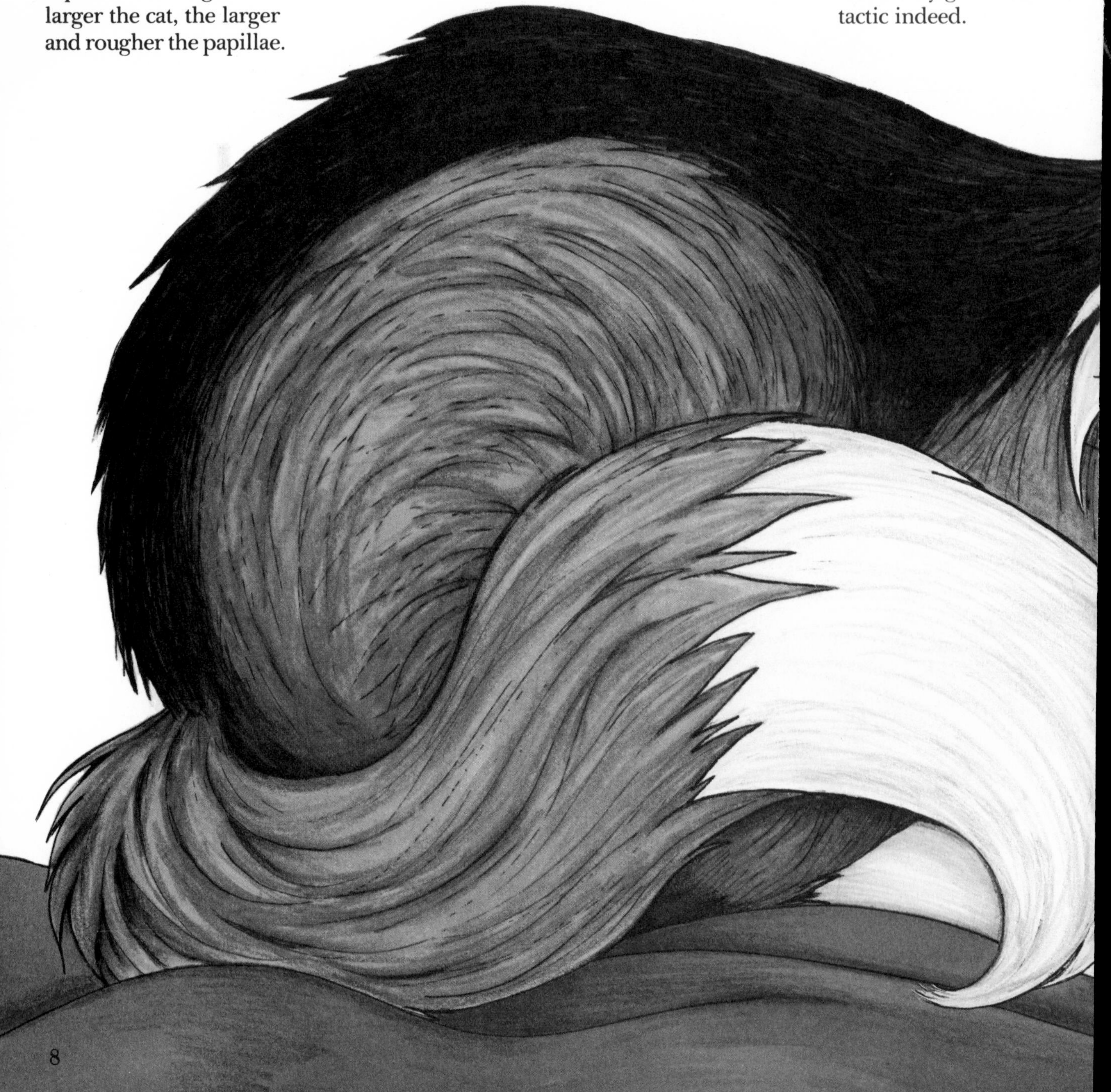

Why do cats have whiskers?

The stiff, wiry whiskers sticking out over a cat's eyes and from the sides of its face, are sensitive feelers. Even the slightest touch on these whiskers sends a message to the cat's brain. Thus a cat knows that if it can squeeze its head through a narrow opening without its whiskers being touched, the rest of its body will probably be able to get through too.

How do cats purr?

Scientists know that most cats purr when they're happy, and that mother cats purr to call their newborn kittens at feeding time. Cats also purr when they're getting a lot of attention, which is probably why your cat may purr on the vet's examination table. But, alas, scientists aren't really sure *how* cats purr.

One theory is that the purring noise is caused by blood rushing through a large, funnel-shaped vein in the cat's chest. When a cat is happy, extra blood flows through this vein, causing it to vibrate where it narrows to pass through the cat's liver and diaphragm. The diaphragm is a muscle stretched tight like a drumskin so it amplifies the vibrations into a low, rumbling sound—purring.

Why does a skunk make such a horrible smell?

A skunk is small—about the size of a large house cat—can't climb very well and doesn't run fast. It hasn't needed to learn how to fight back successfully or even how to escape from a predator. Instead, it makes its enemies run away by squirting a foul-smelling liquid called mercaptan.

A skunk doesn't have to spray its enemies very often because they recognize its bold stripes that warn, "Stay away or I'll spray." It's just as well, because a skunk can only make enough mercaptan to spray five times a week.

Do furry animals get hot in the summer?

Don't feel sorry for your shaggy dog on a hot day. If you stick your hands into its fur, you'll find that the hair close to the skin is much cooler than that at the surface. Sheep beat the heat exactly the same way, but their fleece is one of nature's best insulators. The wool next to their skin can be 5°C/11°F cooler than the wool at the surface.

Why do rabbits hop?

A rabbit has such long, strong hind legs and short front legs that hopping is the fastest and most efficient way to travel. A full-grown white-tailed jack rabbit can hop 64 km ph/40 miles per hour.

How many kinds of animals are there in the world?

There are more than one million kinds of animals that have been identified and scientists are finding many more every year.

Why do dogs' ears prick up when people don't even notice a noise?

Dogs make up for their ho-hum sight with a super sense of hearing. They can hear a noise a block away that a person wouldn't hear if it were right next door. Rover hears almost twice as well as you and about a third better than most cats.

What's the difference between a donkey and a mule?

You might say a donkey is an ass—a domesticated wild ass. It's related to a horse, but has long ears, a large head, a short mane, a tuft of hair on the end of the tail as well as two dark bands on the back and the shoulders.

A mule is the offspring of a female horse and a male donkey. Mules are usually larger, stronger and less nervous than donkeys.

Where did the expression "playing possum" come from?

Even though most people have never seen an opossum, almost everyone knows how to "play possum"—it means not moving, hoping you'll be left alone. And that's exactly what the opossum does when being hunted by its enemies, such as an owl, bobcat or hawk. Curled up on its side with its eyes and mouth open, the opossum looks so lifeless that its enemies soon lose interest, or perhaps lose sight of their prey, and move off in search of a more appetizing dinner. A few minutes later the opossum looks quickly around, gets up and ambles off as if nothing happened.

Although it might seem to be awfully clever of the opossum to pretend to be dead in order to fool its enemies, it is believed that "playing dead" is simply an automatic reaction probably brought on by fear. If it does not play dead it usually defends itself with its teeth.

Do polar bears hibernate?

Only a pregnant polar bear dens up for winter. The temperature inside her snug snow den is about 21°C/70°F warmer than the air outside. She sleeps a lot, but gets up from time to time to adjust the temperature in her ice cave by poking a hole in the roof or closing it up with snow. All polar bears, other than mothers and babies, are loners, wandering summer and winter in search of food, seeking shelter during the most terrible storms. Males and females are together only at mating time, so fathers never see their babies.

Why do bats squeak?

Bats squeak in order to find food and to avoid bumping into things in the dark. A bat, like a whale, makes squeaking noises, which bounce off objects around it, then "hears" the returning sound waves.

Echolocation is such an excellent system for locating things you can't see, it was copied by inventors. Today almost all planes use it: it's called radar.

What do bats look like up close?

Bats are warm-blooded mammals with fur-covered bodies. Their hairless wings are thin membranes of skin stretched between the bones of their very long fingers, their front legs, bodies and back legs.

The largest bat in the world is the flying fox of Malaya. Its wing span is wider than you can stretch your arms. One of the smallest is the North American little brown bat. It would fit into the palm of your hand.

How does a bat catch insects?

A bat that eats insects either catches them in its mouth or uses its wings and tail membranes like a baseball mitt to scoop its dinner out of the air. Not all bats eat insects, however. The large bulldog bat of South America, for example, finds a fish by echolocation, then rakes the water with its claws until it snares its prey; bats in the African tropics often eat fruit.

What do you do if a bat flies into your home?

Simply open the doors and windows, turn off the lights and stay quiet. Remember, a bat can "see" in the dark because of its echolocation system. Be sure not to touch a bat because its bite can make you very sick. If a bat in your house does not fly away on its own, trap it gently between two objects—a piece of stiff cardboard and a food strainer work well, or even two tennis racquets. Then take it outside and let it go.

Who are a bat's main enemies?

A bat's main enemies are human beings. If a bat eats too many insects that have been sprayed with chemicals, the harmful poisons build up in its body until it grows sick or dies. People who explore caves in winter also run the risk of endangering bats that may be hibernating there. There are records of thousands of frightened bats dying because they used up all their energy trying to escape from their caves.

Are bats blind?

Some people may tell you that bats are so blind they can get entangled in your hair. This is not true. Even though bats have very tiny eyes, which are of little use to them at night, they are very good at finding their way in the dark using echolocation. Only a deaf bat would bump into a person's head.

Do bats lay eggs or have babies?

A female bat gives birth to live babies and nurses them with her milk. She usually has only one baby at a time.

Why do bats hang upside down?

Because a bat burns up energy quickly when it's flying, it must save energy whenever possible. If you've ever grown tired of waiting for a parade you know that standing or even sitting burns up energy. That's because your leg and back muscles have to work against the force of gravity to keep your body upright. So when a bat sleeps or hibernates, it simply hangs upside down by its clawed back feet, like a folded umbrella. Much easier!

Why do so many people hate bats?

Sometimes, unfortunately, people fear things they don't know much about. Bats, for example. But the more you learn about bats, the more you can appreciate them.

What's the longest snake in the world?

Both contenders for the world's longest snake are hard to find. The reticulated python of Southeast Asia, Indonesia and the Philippines has been measured at just over 9.7m/32 feet (they're almost always over 6m/20 feet). And there's a report of a Brazilian anaconda stretching in at more than 11.2m/37 feet. Either one would need six beds lying in a row if it wanted to lie down for a nap!

What is the smallest bug?

You need good eyesight to watch a flea circus. But to watch a circus of hairy-winged beetles and fairy flies performing, you'd also need a very strong magnifying glass. These little insects are much smaller than the period at the end of this sentence.

What's the coldest place on earth?

If you go down to Vostock, Antarctica, take thermal underwear, a down vest, jacket and parka and loads of mittens. The place is usually about −57.8°C/−72°F. In July, the average temperature can drop to −90°C/−130°F.

The hottest place, in case you want to know that too, is Dallol, Ethiopia, near the southern end of the Red Sea. The maximum daily temperature recorded for 10 months of the year is 37.8°C/100°F. It cools down in December and January, though, to an average of 36.7°C/98°F.

What animal weighs the most?

The all-time heavyweight champ is the blue whale. It can weigh more than 16 large elephants, or 1,600 grown men or women.

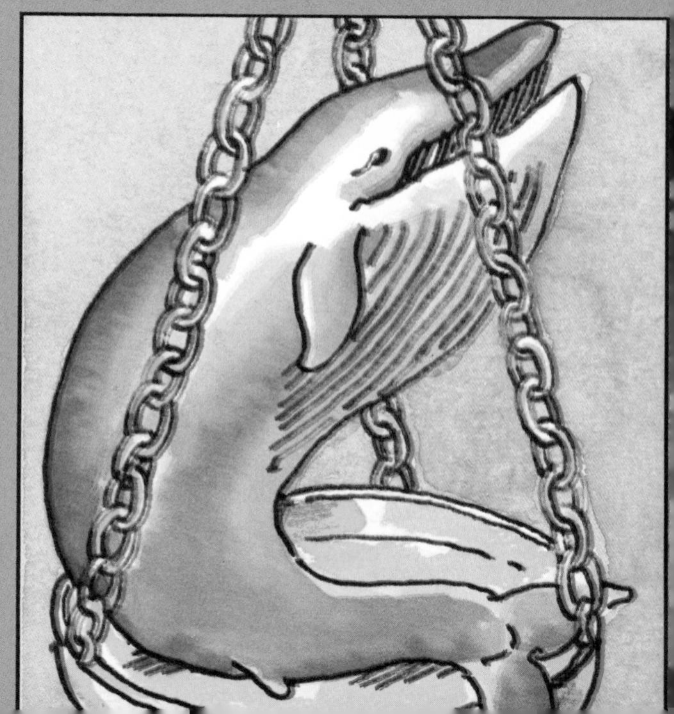

Vhat's the largest flower?

)ne rafflesia arnoldi flower would make a whole ouquet. Its white and orange-brown blossom is about ie size of an umbrella. Perhaps you're wondering vhat kind of plant can hold up a blossom that big? 'his Southeast Asian monster flower attaches itself) jungle vines. The vines have to be strong, because single blossom can weigh as much as a fat cat.

Vhat's the biggest bird egg ever laid?

3efore it became extinct in the mid-1600s, the :lephant bird that flew the skies over Madagascar produced the biggest eggs scientists have ever liscovered. These eggs were as big as breadboxes, ıbout two-thirds bigger than those laid by an ostrich. The elephant bird's eggshells were so amazingly trong that they were often used as water jugs once he egg white and yolk had been drained out.

What's the biggest bird?

The average male North African ostrich is so tall that he would bump his head walking in your front door. While ostriches may be large, they are not very brave: if they sense danger, they usually choose to run away.

Why does your mouth water when you smell food?

As soon as you smell food, your computerlike brain automatically remembers if it's something you like. It then gets you ready to eat by sending a message to your mouth: "Start the saliva flowing." What's saliva? It's a special fluid that does several important things. It mixes with food to make it easier for you to swallow, and it starts breaking down food and turning it into fuel.

Why and how fast do we blink?

Have you ever tried to outstare someone? It's difficult to do because you've got to force yourself to stop blinking—something you do thousands of times each day without even noticing. If you stopped blinking altogether, you'd probably go blind. That's because the delicate outer covering of your eyeballs would dry out and become infected. Also, blinking washes cleansing tears over your eyeballs to get rid of dust and dirt. So keep on blinking. After all, a blink of the eye takes only 300 milliseconds—much faster than it takes you to think about it!

Why does peeling onions make you cry?

When you peel an onion, a very powerful acid escapes into the air. If some of this acid reaches your eyes, they try to wash it away with tears. How can you avoid crying over an onion? Well, if you don't mind how silly you look, you could wear skin-diving goggles when you're peeling one. Or hold the onion under water as you peel it.

Vhy do people blush?

'eople blush in threatening situations. These could nclude when someone makes fun of you or threatens o punch you in the nose. Here's how it all happens.)ne part of your brain sends a chemical "message" o another part we'll call the "control center" telling t to get your body ready to defend itself. This means nore blood will be needed in your muscles. You don't ıormally notice the extra blood that rushes to, say, 'our legs or biceps, but you do notice when it reaches 'our face. It happens automatically, so there's ıothing you can do to stop a blush once it starts.

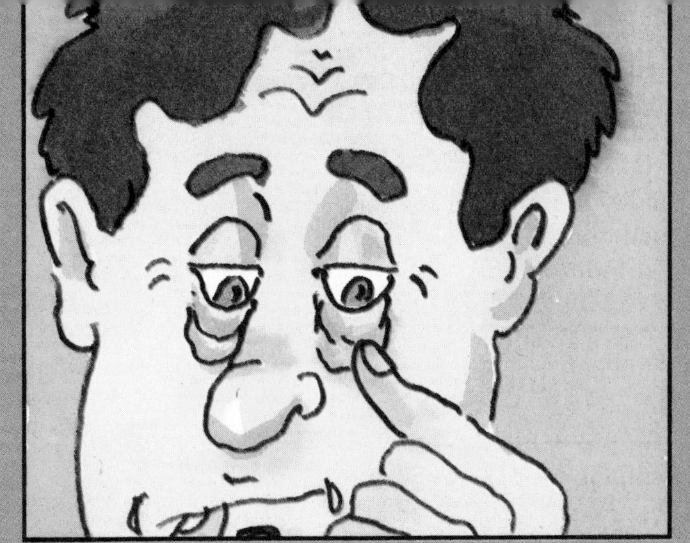

Why do people get circles under their eyes when they're tired?

If you could board a tiny boat to travel inside your body, you'd sail along arteries or veins. Your arteries swoosh oxygen-rich, red blood from your heart and lungs to all parts of your body. Your veins sluggishly carry old, used-up, bluish-colored blood back to your heart and lungs, where it is freshened up again. When a person is tired, the entire system that feeds blood into the veins slows down and gets backed up. So what about those dark circles? They're nothing more than old, tired blood lying in the backed-up veins waiting to get back to the heart.

Why do we get butterflies in our stomach?

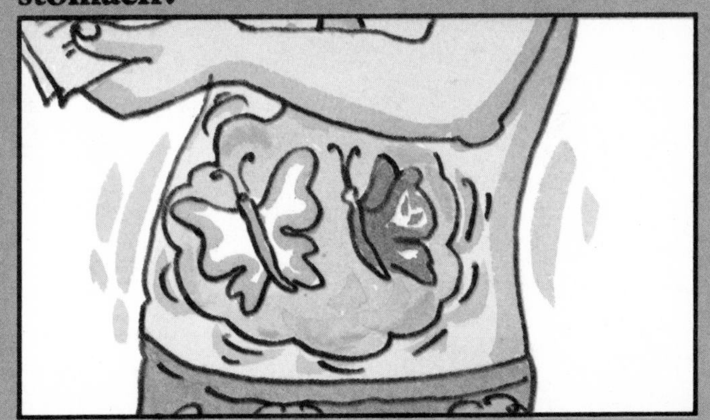

Your stomach is slowly moving all the time to digest or "break down" the food you put into it. When you're nervous, however, your brain directs your stomach to "change gears"—to stop digesting food. It does this to conserve energy so the other muscles in your body will have more energy for whatever action you'll have to take: fighting, fleeing or even reciting a poem in front of the class. Unfortunately, as your stomach changes gears, its smooth movement is disrupted. That's when you feel as if three or four butterflies are flip-flopping around trying to get out.

Why do we get dizzy when we spin around?

Chances are when you spin around you get more than dizzy! Try this trick: Turn on the radio or play a record. Stand in the middle of the room, making sure that there are no chairs or tables near by. Close your eyes, cover up one ear and spin yourself around 10 times. Keeping your eyes closed, stop; try to point to the radio or record. Chances are you not only got dizzy, but were fooled as to where the sound was coming from.

Why? When you spin with your eyes closed, you become disoriented. But the problem of losing your balance and locating the sound wrongly also has to do with your ears. Human ears have two kinds of nerves to send messages to the brain. One controls balance, the other controls sound. These nerves are in a liquid base. When you spin, this liquid spins too, and hence the messages that go to your brain get all mixed up, even after spinning for just a moment or two. So your brain continues to receive messages that you're turning even when you're not. Whew!

If you stare at something, why can you sometimes still see it even when you look away?

If you stare hard at, say, a red square for one minute and look quickly away at a white wall or a blank piece of paper, you'll still "see" the square for a few seconds. This happens because you were concentrating so hard on the square that its image became strongly "fixed" in your brain. It keeps remembering the image even after you shifted your eyes. You fooled your brain.

Why do people shrink when they get old?

People don't really "shrink" when they get old. Granny just appears to be getting smaller, and this happens for a variety of reasons. If you slouch, the gristle along your backbone tightens up, which eventually makes it increasingly difficult to stand tall. As you age, your bones tend to become weaker and thinner and this also gives you the appearance of "shrinking."

Why don't some old people remember things?

How your brain remembers things is still baffling physiologists. When you are born, your brain is developing. As you mature, it continues to grow, allowing you to store more and more bits of information there. As you go through life and experience different things, it all gets coded in your brain. An active mind can retrieve these memories easily, although no one is really sure how.

As you grow, your brain keeps growing too, until it reaches its maximum capacity in your late teens. At that time, it's crammed with 10 zillion (10^{12}) neurons where information can be stored. But then thousands of neurons begin to be destroyed every day. And since these neurons are never replaced, your brain's capacity eventually declines.

There's little one can do to stop memory loss from happening, although exercise is important. It keeps blood flowing to the brain.

How do you taste things?

Tasting chocolate, lemon, potato chips or anything else puts not only your tongue to work, but also your nose and eyes.

If you don't believe that you need your eyes, nose and tongue to taste, try this trick on some friends: Cut equal-sized pieces of raw peeled potato, apple and radish. Blindfold your friends and ask them to hold their noses. Then have them taste the potato, the apple and the radish. They won't know which food is which.

Why? Because there wasn't enough information for their brains to tell them what they were eating. Anyone who has ever had a cold knows this too. When you're all stuffed up, food doesn't have any taste.

What happens when you sneeze?

Sneezing protects your lungs. When dust sneaks past the cleaning system in your nose and throat, an alarm goes off in your brain. The tubes leading to your lungs quickly narrow so that the dust "invader" can't squeeze through them. Of course, when you try to breathe out, you can't because your tubes are no longer wide enough. Soon the pressure becomes too great and—achoo—your tubes are blasted open by an explosion of air traveling as fast as a World Series' pitch!

Why doesn't it tickle when you tickle yourself?

When someone else tickles you, a fast message is sent from your skin to your brain. Your brain quickly makes you react—you laugh, or scream and pull away. If you tickle yourself, your brain does not bother to make you respond because it knows that it's in control of the tickler.

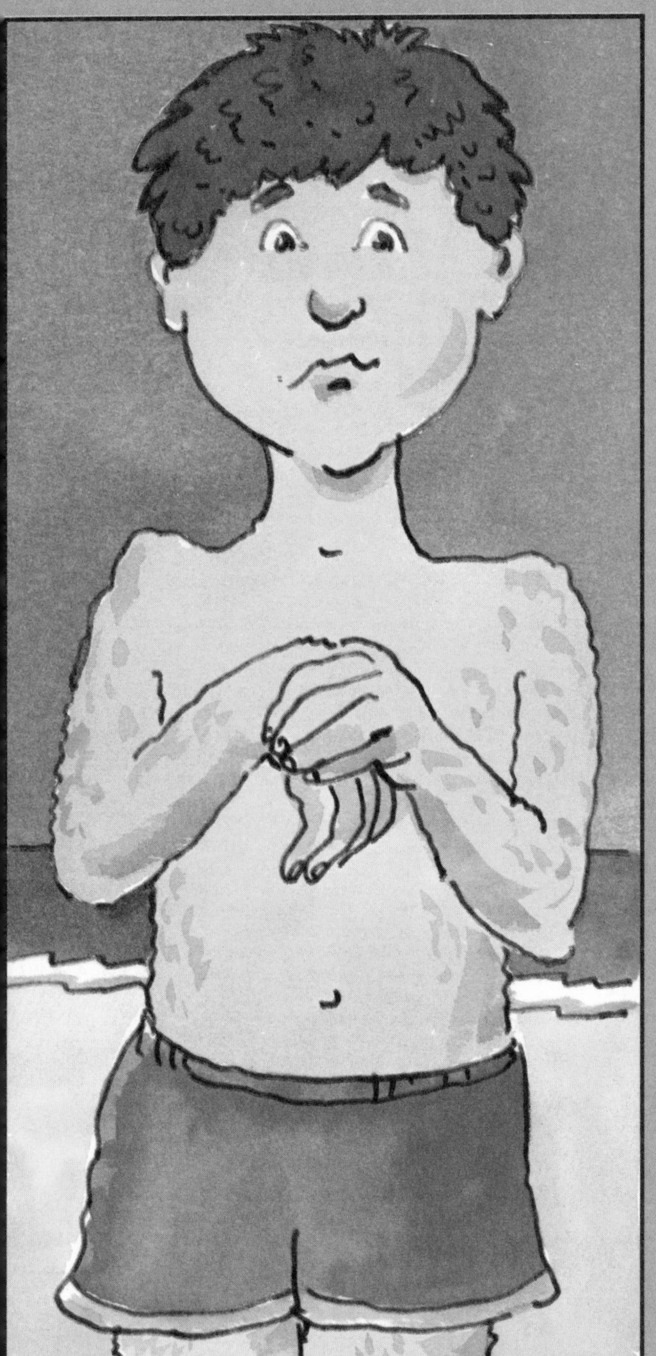

What are goose bumps?

When the skin on your arms and legs looks like the bumpy skin of a freshly plucked goose, you'll know that your brain is trying to warm you up. At the base of the thousands of little hairs that cover your body are tiny muscles. When these muscles tense, they make your hair stand on end. This traps a layer of air close to your skin, where it can be warmed by your body. The bumps you see are the little muscles straining to hold up each hair. It's easy to see why you get goose bumps when you're cold, but what about when you're scared? Your brain is warming up your muscles in case you need to fight or run away.

Where do tears come from?

Behind your eyelids, at the outer edge of your eyes, are small glands called lacrimal glands. They are continuously at work, making fluid to squirt into your eyes, keeping them moist and clean. When you cry, these glands work overtime so tears flow out drainage holes into your nose, making you sniffle. Your nose isn't running—your glands are dripping.

Why does skin shrivel up when you stay in bath water too long?

You get "prune fingers" and even "prune feet" when your skin dries out. It might seem odd to you that your skin can become dry and wrinkly when you're sitting up to your neck in bath water, but it works like this. Soapy water, especially, robs your skin of its protective coating of oil. This allows water inside your skin to slowly ooze out into the bath water, so your skin is actually drying from the inside out. When your skin has lost too much water, some of its cells collapse, forming wrinkles.

What are UFOs?

A UFO (unidentified flying object) is anything in the sky that's unexplained and behaves in a way that seems unusual. Many things average people see in the sky are unexplained and, therefore, are called UFOs. However, to an astronomer or a meteorologist, these same things might have a logical explanation. They might be airplanes, or research balloons reflecting sunlight, or the planet Venus, whose light can be distorted by heat waves in the atmosphere.

Some scientists think that all UFO sightings (it's estimated that there are at least 100 reported world-wide every day) can be explained in such simple terms. Others think they cannot and insist that there are many reports that remain unexplained even after investigation by experts. One of their possible explanations for UFOs is that they are flying saucers; another is that they are some kind of weather or atmospheric event, such as ball lightning, which appears as if from nowhere and then disappears. Yet another idea is that UFOs exist only in the mind of the person seeing them. Think about that!

How long have people been seeing UFOs?

Most of the sightings of UFOs have been made in the last 30 years. However, reports of strange objects in the sky can be found in the Bible and many other writings from hundreds and hundreds of years ago. Sightings are made in every country by all types of people, including such highly trained technicians as pilots and engineers.

What are planets?

By definition, a planet is any large body in our solar system that orbits around the sun. The Earth is a planet, and there are eight others. In order, they are Mercury, Venus, Earth, Mars, Jupiter, Saturn, Uranus, Neptune and Pluto. The orbits are rather like rings around a bull's eye, with the bull's eye being the sun. Mercury orbits closest to the sun, Pluto the farthest away (although sometimes it gets inside Neptune's orbit). Jupiter is the largest planet, 12 times the diameter of the Earth. Pluto is the smallest — smaller than Earth's moon.

It is possible that beyond Pluto, but still in our solar system, there is a planet bigger than the Earth, or that other stars like the sun could have planets, but we haven't discovered them because they are so far away.

Why is Venus called our twin planet?

Venus is a dead planet of scorched brown rock. Above the Venusian ground swirls a soupy, orange smog topped by poisonous clouds of sulfuric acid that are swept around the planet nonstop by strong winds. It might seem hard to understand why people call this our twin planet.

Venus was named our twin partly because it's the same size as Earth and is our next-door neighbor in the solar system. But recently scientists have begun to wonder if Venus was once much more like Earth than it is today— complete with rivers, streams and maybe even vegetation.

Venus is closer to the sun than Earth is. Some new theories suggest that this closeness to the sun caused Venus to heat up billions of years ago. The oceans evaporated there boosting the carbon dioxide in the Venusian atmosphere. This increased carbon dioxide made the atmosphere thicker so that it trapped even more heat. Once this happened, the planet became so hot that all possibility of life died. But before all scientists can accept this theory about our now-unalike twin, much more must be known.

If you visited a planet with several moons, could you see them all in the sky at the same time?

The planets Mars, Jupiter, Saturn, Uranus and Neptune all have more than one moon, although some of them are very small. If you were to travel to Jupiter you'd find it an exciting place to look for moons. Four of Jupiter's moons would look somewhat the same as our one moon and there would be times when all four could be seen at once, each in a different phase. But the best place of all for moon-watching would be Saturn. If you looked into the sky from Saturn on a clear night, you might see at least five of Saturn's seven moons.

Why do birds have feathers?

Bird feathers serve two purposes. First, when fluffed up, feathers trap air that helps to keep the bird warm. Your down-filled jacket works just the same way. Feathers are also essential for flying. Wing feathers help to get the bird up into the air. Tail feathers steer a bird through the sky and keep it balanced on the ground.

Why do birds preen their feathers?

When a bird turns its head around and nuzzles its feathers with its beak, it's said to be preening. You don't have to wait long to see a bird preening its feathers—it does it often, and not just because it wants to look beautiful.

When a bird preens, it takes a beakful of water-repellent oil from a preen gland right above the base of the tail and smooths the oil over its feathers. This makes the feathers waterproof. Feathers that aren't waterproofed get waterlogged, which makes the bird too heavy to fly.

Preening not only oils feathers, it keeps them smooth and removes bugs and dirt. Since dirty feathers let out body heat, unkempt feathers can make flying difficult and feathers that are full of parasites can make a bird sick, preening is a good habit.

Why do birds sing?

Birds sing to attract a mate and to establish their territory. They also chatter to one another. In winter this chattering is quite important. Individual members of a flock of birds—chickadees, for example—give "recognition calls." If a strange bird tries to join the flock or share their feeder but can't give the right call to show it belongs within the flock, the other birds will attack and peck the intruder until it flies away.

How do birds breathe?

Birds need up to 20 times more oxygen when they are flying than when they're resting. They could breathe hard and fast to get enough, but we know they don't. Instead, birds recycle air to get as much oxygen as possible out of each breath and to get rid of the carbon dioxide as quickly as possible. Connected to a bird's lungs are five air sacs. Air that's been through the lungs is stored in these sacs for a fraction of a second, then sent back to the lungs. By recycling each breath in this way, birds squeeze every bit of oxygen they can out of the air they breathe, without wasting energy by breathing twice as fast.

Why don't birds fall off branches when they sleep?

Perching birds have a handy way of staying upright when they settle down to sleep. Because a perching bird has ankles that bend backward and downward, it can clamp its toes tightly around a branch. The bird's weight presses downward, locking the toes and legs in this position. When the bird wants to fly away, it simply straightens its ankles and takes off.

If penguins are birds, why can't they fly?

The penguin is as graceful a flyer as any bird. But it flies not in the air, but in the sea. There it flaps its wings very quickly, just like an air-flying bird, to propel itself through the water. It's so well streamlined that it can even do "dolphin leaps" over and under the water. Penguins stopped air flying many millions of years ago and their wings became rigid, boardlike and too small to support their weight in the air. But they're great paddlers, both underwater and on ice and snow—"tobogganing" is a favorite penguin pastime.

Vhy are penguins black and white?

'here are two possible dvantages to the enguin's black and vhite suit. First, it makes he bird very difficult to e seen in the water. A redator looking down rom the sky probably an't see the penguin's lark back in the black lepths of the sea; and redators swimming below would probably miss the bird's light belly against the sunlight-dappled water.

The second reason is warmth. Since black absorbs heat, black backs help to keep penguins warm. If they're cold, penguins turn their backs to the sun; if they're hot, they face it.

How do penguins keep warm?

A penguin doesn't worry about the cold because it wears four layers of "clothes." Under its thick skin is an even thicker layer of fat, like blubber, which helps to keep heat in its body. And at the base of its oily, tightly-packed, water-proofed feathers are tufts of down that help trap air around the penguin's body. It's a bit like wearing a down jacket, a sweater, thermal underwear and a wet suit.

No matter how long a penguin stays underwater its skin never gets wet. That's because its feathers overlap as tightly as fish scales. There are 22 feathers per dime-sized space on a penguin's skin.

In really cold weather, adult emperor penguins form "huddles" to conserve body heat. Sometimes up to 6,000 penguins stand close together while they incubate their eggs.

How do birds know when to start migrating?

Many birds start to head south before the weather gets really cold. But how do they know winter is coming? It's not simply a question of dwindling food supplies. Could it be that they tell the season is about to change by noticing the shortening fall days? Scientists have experimented with wild birds in large cages, gradually shortening the days by turning off electric lights. They discovered that the birds' awareness of the fewer daylight hours caused them to head to the south side of their cage! It was as if they were trying to begin their migration.

And why do birds migrate? The fact that some birds do not migrate gives us an important clue. Birds whose food supplies are not destroyed by cold or covered by snow, such as many woodpeckers or chickadees (which eat larvae or eggs that are on or in tree trunks), needn't migrate because they can find food even during the long winter months. But birds that depend on grain, shoots, insects and other foods that cannot be found in winter have to migrate—or starve.

The tiny ruby-throated hummingbird, for example, travels all the way from Canada to Mexico each winter searching for nectar to drink from flowers. Why doesn't it stay wher it's warm all year? Well, one little hummingbird might not need much food, but if all the hummingbirds in Nortl America decided never to leave sunny Mexico, the nectar supply would soon run low. By migrating north again, hummingbirds never run out of food.

Do birds have teeth?

Most birds don't have teeth, but they can still "chew" their food. They swallow little bits of dirt and small stones that rattle around in their gizzard (part of the stomach) and in this way grind up their food. If you feed birds when there's lots of snow on the ground, add crushed egg shells to the bird feed because it might be difficult for birds to finc little bits of stone.

Even when a bird is full, it doesn't have to stop eating. At the top o its stomach is a bag callec a crop. When the gizzarc is full, extra food is storec in the crop. If a bird wants to enjoy a meal in safety and at leisure it will often fill its crop anc digest the food later.

When birds migrate, how do they know how to get there?

Birds, it seems, are better navigators than human beings. Scientists still do not fully understand how birds know which direction to head, but it is thought that they use the sun as a compass. To take an accurate bearing from the sun, however, they must also know the time of day since the sun moves to a different place in the sky as the day progresses.

Birds also use stars to find their way on their long flights. But some birds can navigate without any help from either the sun or stars. The homing pigeon is one example. It can fly straight home, even on very cloudy days. How? Scientists think that the earth's magnetic field guides some birds, but they are still trying to find out how.

How can birds fly?

If you have ever held a bird in your hand, you know that it has a very light body. This is because it has hollow bones and air sacs near its lungs. A bird also has very strong wing muscles. Put all these features together and you've got an incredible flying machine. As the bird's wings flap down, the long outer feathers close and push against the air, lifting the bird up, while the feathers on the wingtip pull the bird forward. As the bird's wings go up, the long outer feathers open so that the air can pass between them, while the wingtip feathers push back against the air to keep the bird moving ahead. Birds such as ostriches, of course, don't fly. They tend to have heavy bones, all the better to support their weight as they walk around on land.

Did dragons ever really exist?

The dragons in our storybooks exist only in the minds of people, but they've been lurking there for thousands of years. Some of the oldest tales about dragons are the wildest. For example, would you believe that dragons were fond of cooling themselves on hot days by drinking chilled elephants' blood?

Where did people get all their odd ideas about dragons? No one knows, but whoever first saw a giant lizard leap out of underbrush on the South Pacific island of Komodo must have thought he had seen a storybook dragon in the flesh.

Komodo dragons, which weigh more than a full refrigerator and are almost twice as long, lumber around on legs as thick as tree trunks and feed on wild pigs, deer and water buffalo. And like their distant snake relatives, they sometime swallow prey whole. Komodo dragons have been seen gulping down a pig, then walking off with their bellies dragging on the ground

Is it true that crocodiles cry?

When somebody says a person is shedding crocodile tears, he or she means that person is pretending to be sad. This expression began because some people once believed that crocodiles cried to make their victims come closer to see what was the matter. It is now known that crocodiles do cry, but for physical, rather than emotional reasons. Their kidneys are unable to get rid of all the salt that crocodiles take in, so glands in their head extract the salt and pass it out as tears.

Penguins and other seabirds that eat salty food and drink mostly salt water also must rid their bodies of salt, so they too have salt glands above their eyes. Their tears dribble down their bills and away.

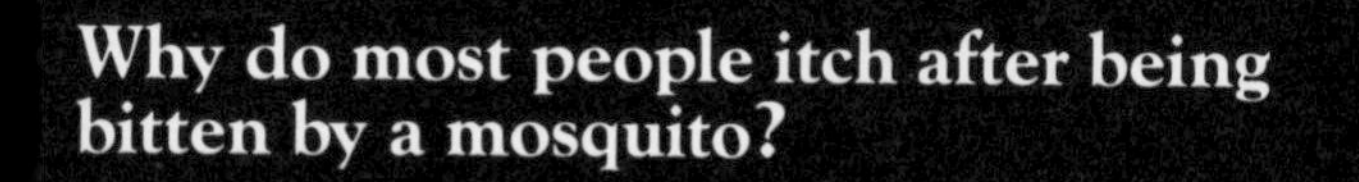

Why do most people itch after being bitten by a mosquito?

If you itch after being bitten by a mosquito, it's because you're allergic to a chemical the mosquito injects into you with its saliva to keep your blood from clotting. Depending on how sensitive you are, this chemical, called histamine, can cause the swelling and itching to last for days.

No one knows why some people attract more mosquitoes than others, but here are a couple of tricks that may help to reduce your chances of a bite. Because mosquitoes appear to be attracted by dark colors and rough textures, wear pale yellow or white. A smooth textured, pale outfit will be much less attractive to a mosquito than jeans. Another trick is to not wear perfume or after shave lotion or, for that matter, to shampoo your hair. No one knows why but certain scents also seem to be alluring to mosquitoes.

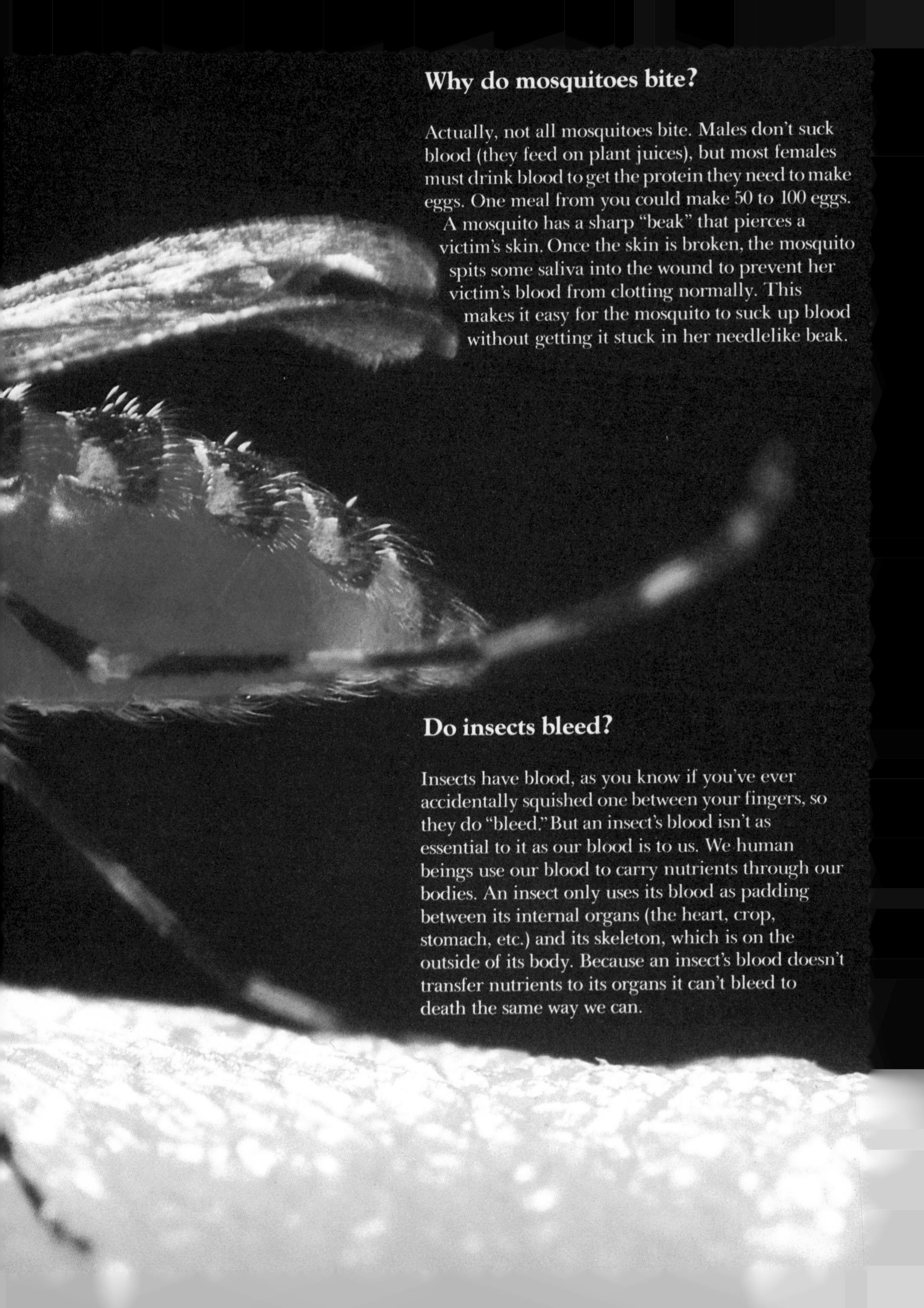

Why do mosquitoes bite?

Actually, not all mosquitoes bite. Males don't suck blood (they feed on plant juices), but most females must drink blood to get the protein they need to make eggs. One meal from you could make 50 to 100 eggs.

A mosquito has a sharp "beak" that pierces a victim's skin. Once the skin is broken, the mosquito spits some saliva into the wound to prevent her victim's blood from clotting normally. This makes it easy for the mosquito to suck up blood without getting it stuck in her needlelike beak.

Do insects bleed?

Insects have blood, as you know if you've ever accidentally squished one between your fingers, so they do "bleed." But an insect's blood isn't as essential to it as our blood is to us. We human beings use our blood to carry nutrients through our bodies. An insect only uses its blood as padding between its internal organs (the heart, crop, stomach, etc.) and its skeleton, which is on the outside of its body. Because an insect's blood doesn't transfer nutrients to its organs it can't bleed to death the same way we can.

What are an insect's wings made of?

Most insects have two pairs of wings—a forewing and a hindwing—on each side of their body. (Some have only one pair of wings and others are wingless.) Insect wings are usually membranous, which means they are very thin, almost transparent, like cellophane. Some wings look thick and leathery, others are hairy and still others are scalelike, but underneath them all you'll usually discover the same membranous material.

Wings are made up of veins and cells (a cell being the empty space between the veins). When an insect hatches, it immediately pumps blood into the veins in its wings. When this happens, the wings expand almost like balloons to their full adult size.

Why do moths like light?

No one really knows why moths are attracted by electric or ultraviolet light. Some scientists believe this is because moths use moonlight to guide themselves at night. A porch light confuses them and because they are confused, they fly around in circles.

Flying around artificial lights at night is a dangerous thing for moths to do because it makes it easy for such enemies as bats and toads to spot them.

Many moths aren't attracted to light at all. And for some reason, females seldom come near an electric light until after they've laid their eggs.

What's the difference between moth and butterfly caterpillars?

Both moth and butterfly caterpillars begin as tiny eggs laid by their mothers on a leaf. When the eggs hatch into caterpillars, you can hardly tell the difference.

Both moth and butterfly caterpillars feed on the leaves of trees and grow and grow. As they do, they shed their skin several times. Each time this happens a creature wriggles out that still looks like a caterpillar.

After five sheddings, or molts, the last larval skin comes off and the caterpillars go into a new stage of their life: the pupal stage. Now differences begin to appear. Both moth and butterfly caterpillars spin out a small ball of silk from a special gland in their bodies, and use this ball to attach their hind end to a leaf or plant stem.

A butterfly caterpillar may also spin a line of silk around the middle of its body to anchor it more securely in place.

The moth caterpillar usually then spins enough silk to completely surround its body. Once it's covered in this light, strong silk ball, the moth caterpillar is said to be in a cocoon.

Most butterfly caterpillars don't spin cocoons, but they too are protected from the wind, cold and enemies. Beneath the butterfly caterpillar's last molt is a hard chrysalis case.

Both the chrysalis and the cocoon seem to hang there quietly, but inside a great drama is happening. Within weeks, months or over the winter (depending on the species), the caterpillar changes form. What breaks out will be an adult butterfly or moth.

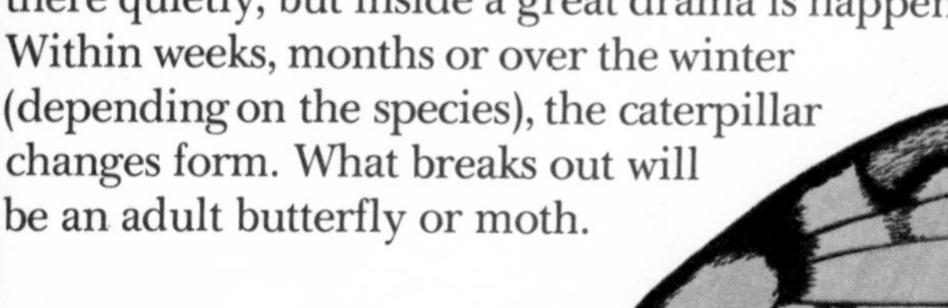

How can you tell the difference between a moth and a butterfly?

Moths tend to hide by day and fly by night. Seeing them in the daytime is often difficult because they are well camouflaged so birds can't find them as they rest on tree trunks or leaves. But if you do find one, you'll probably discover it has a thick, hairy body and often feathery, fernlike antennae.

Butterflies, which do fly during the day, are not generally as hairy or woolly as moths and tend to be more brightly colored. At the tips of their long, slim feelers or antennae, butterflies often have little decorative knobs.

If you're still not certain whether you're seeing a butterfly or a moth, look at the way it rests. Generally a moth will sit with its wings laid out flat while a butterfly will fold its wings up over its back.

Why do fish swim in schools?

Scientists aren't completely sure why some fish swim in schools. But they do know that there is never a leader or a "teacher" and that some fish schools are very small, having as few as three members—while others can have as many as 1,000 fish.

It is believed that fish swim in schools for protection. The larger the school, the less chance any one individual has of being eaten. If a fish school is threatened, its members often move closer together as if trying to hide behind one another. And it works. The big fish attacking gets confused by the crowd of little fish swimming this way and that. It's like trying to play tennis with several balls at the same time.

Schools of fish have developed several other group tactics for darting away from predators. If a big fish sneaks up from behind, the school might split into two groups, turn and swim around behind it, then regroup again. That leaves the predator wondering where his prey went. If a big fish attacks from the side, the little fish scatter in all directions, which also confuses the predator. It all proves that, for fish, there's definitely safety in numbers.

Do fish sleep?

Most fish spend part of each 24-hour period "asleep." Being asleep to a fish, however, can mean anything from simply slowing down all movement while still being aware of what's going on around, to losing consciousness completely, as humans do when they sleep. Open-water fish, such as herring or tuna, hang motionless in the water at night. Some fresh-water fish, such as catfish, find a log or river bank to shelter under during the day. Other fresh-water fish, such as perch, often hide under overhanging rocks during the night. Still others, such as rockfish and grouper, don't appear to sleep at all, but instead rest against rocks, bracing themselves with their fins. And in case you're wondering, fish don't close their eyes to sleep. They can't. They don't have eyelids.

How do fish stop in water?

A fish uses its dorsal fin for stability, rather like the keel on a boat, to keep it from rolling over; its pelvic and pectoral fins for steering; and its tail fin to propel itself along. When a fish wants to slow down or stop, it spreads out its two pairs of pelvic and pectoral fins almost like a parachute dragging in the water. Then it relaxes and coasts to a stop.

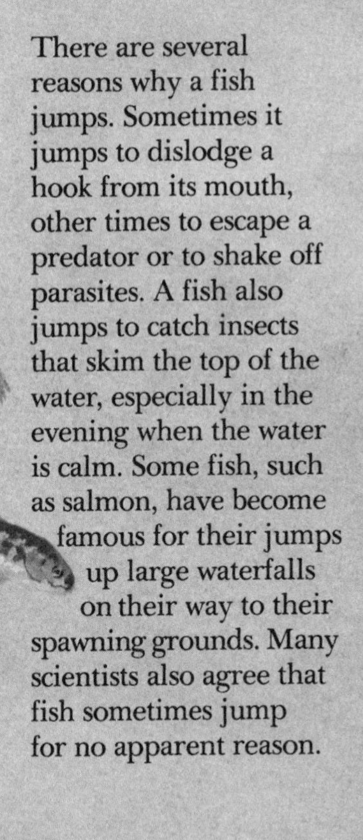

Why do fish jump?

There are several reasons why a fish jumps. Sometimes it jumps to dislodge a hook from its mouth, other times to escape a predator or to shake off parasites. A fish also jumps to catch insects that skim the top of the water, especially in the evening when the water is calm. Some fish, such as salmon, have become famous for their jumps up large waterfalls on their way to their spawning grounds. Many scientists also agree that fish sometimes jump for no apparent reason.

Can fish hear?

Fish hear in different ways. A few fish *feel* sound vibrations, just as we feel bass notes on a sound system, but most don't have eardrums like ours. Instead, they hear through their sides, where they have a line of pores called the "lateral line." These pores respond to pressure changes just as our eardrums do. The pores sense any movement in the water so, for example, fish know if a person or another fish is swimming nearby.

Some fish, the catfish, the midshipman and the Atlantic cod, for example, have inner ears as well. These fish tend to make buzzing or purring noises during courtship or when they are staking out their territory, guarding their eggs or in danger. Scientists believe that a fish that makes noise can hear it.

What are fish scales?

A typical fish body is covered with thin, bony scales that overlap like roof shingles to protect a fish's skin. As a fish grows, its scales increase in size and lost scales are replaced. You can often tell how old a fish is by counting the growth ridges on its scales.

Scales are different depending on the fish. Some fish, such as the freshwater turbot, have very small, delicate scales, while the tarpon which lives in the ocean and the Australian lungfish have scales that are bigger than the size of a quarter. A few fish, such as catfish, have no scales at all.

How can alligators keep their eyes open underwater?

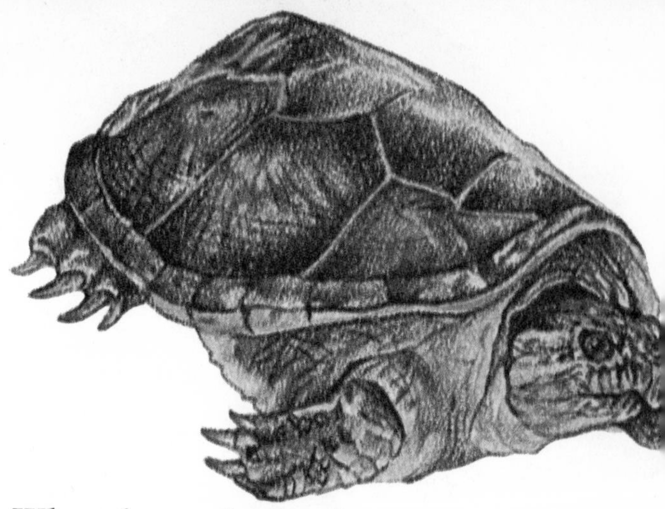

An alligator is very cleverly built for lying around in the water, which it likes to do. Its eyes and nostrils are on the top of its head so that it can breathe and also look around. When an alligator dives, it battens down its hatches like a submarine. Two flaps of muscle in each nostril clamp shut so the water doesn't flood its nose. Other muscle flaps close off an alligator's ears like internal earmuffs. Then it puts on its "goggles," a special transparent third eyelid that is only used underwater. No water can get through, and the eyelid is clear enough for the alligator to see where it's going.

How do you tell the difference between an alligator and a crocodile?

Fortunately you don't have to go too near to tell the difference. The alligator is the one with the broad head and rounded snout, while the crocodile is slimmer and has a long, narrow head and pointed snout. Also, crocodiles tend to be somewhat lighter in color.

If you are up close, there is another way to tell the difference. When its mouth is closed, none of an alligator's teeth stick out. But when a crocodile's mouth is closed, its long fourth side tooth on the lower jaw can be seen pointing up.

What do turtles eat?

A turtle eats whatever's in front of its beak. Some eat fish and water animals; others eat insects, worms and bits of dead animals; and some eat both plant and animal food. There are even some vegetarian turtles.

Some turtles start out life eating meat, which helps them to grow faster. In old age, however, the same turtle may be quite content to munch only on plants.

Turtles' eating habits are unusual in another way: with the exception of land turtles and snapping turtles, most will only swallow underwater.

What's the difference between frogs and toads?

The most obvious difference between these two amphibians is their skin. A frog's skin is smooth and damp, a toad's, dry and very bumpy. A frog's skin dries out easily so the frog needs to stay near ponds or lakes. Dryness doesn't bother toads, so they can stray farther from the water.

Another difference between frogs and toads is their body shape. Toads have squat, chunky bodies and shorter hind legs than frogs. Thus they move more slowly and can't jump as far. Some toads you'll see only at night or if you look in a hole, crevice or burrow. Frogs hop about by day and sing during the evening. They love light and sun, so you'll see many basking on lily pads.

How do chameleons change color?

A chameleon's body is covered with different-colored tiny holes that can be opened or closed by small muscles in the chameleon's skin. When a chameleon wants to hide on a green leaf, it somehow tells some pores to close down so that the red and yellow pigments in the chameleon's skin disappear. That leaves the chameleon looking like part of the leaf. If you watch a chameleon "changing color," you can see that as certain pigments increase or decrease in visibility, it looks as if there's a dye moving through the body. This is not the case. The colors are all there at all times. It's just that some are chosen to be displayed and others are not. A chameleon really knows what it means to "choose your colors."

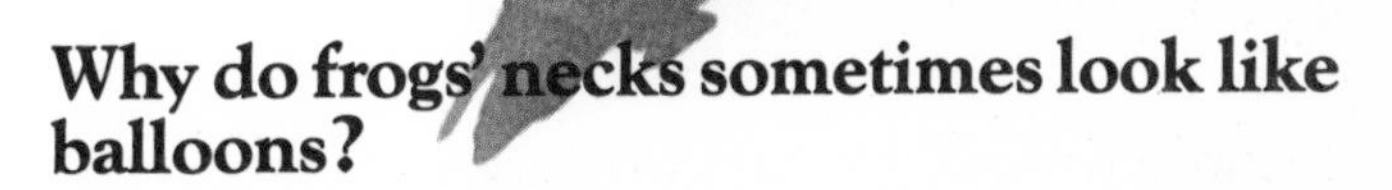

Why do frogs' necks sometimes look like balloons?

The frogs you see with balloonlike pouches under their chins or sticking out from the sides of their heads are males. All that puffed-up display, plus the loud songs that they sing, are simply to impress the females. Some types of frogs link up with their mate through a "female choice breeding system," which means female frogs choose their favorite singers to mate with. Each male produces its own distinctive call. Keeping its nose and mouth firmly shut, the frog forces air up and down between the mouth and the lungs. Some of this air is forced through the floor of the mouth into an air sac that inflates, and the sound can be heard farther away than a frog can hop in a day. When a lady frog likes what she hears, she swims over to her mate and lets him know that he's the one.

Where does the water go when the tide goes out?

Did you guess that it rushes over to the far shore? Well, it doesn't. It rises up into an enormous bulge that is spread out over such a wide area you wouldn't be able to see it even if you were sitting in a satellite directly over the ocean. If you sat beside a pail of water at the beach you wouldn't be able to see the water bulge up in the pail, either, because that area is too small. Scientists, however, have been able to prove that the water bulges by using satellites equipped with remote sensing devices. These devices that measure the distance between the water and the satellite detect even the slightest height variation in the water below.

Why does this bulge happen? The answer has to do with the moon. The moon's gravity, acting like a powerful magnet, pulls the water on the side of the earth that's closest to the moon into a bulge. And because the earth turns in a complete circle during every 24-hour period, this water bulge moves across the earth's surface. When the bulge meets land, it makes a high tide; when it's far away from land, it causes a low tide.

Amazing though it seems, when it's high tide on one side of the earth it's also high tide on the other side of the earth. How? It sounds unbelievable, but while the moon is busy pulling water toward it on one side of the earth, it's also pulling the earth away from the water—on the opposite side.

How can you tell how far away a thunderstorm is?

To find out how far away a thunderstorm is, count the number of seconds between the lightning flash and the sound of thunder and divide by three. This will tell you approximately how many kilometers away the lightning struck. (If it's miles you're more comfortable with, divide by five.) If the flash and the thunder happen together, you won't need any math to tell you that the storm is directly overhead. Your ears will be ringing from the tremendous crack.

What are lightning and thunder?

When you see a flash of lightning dart across the sky, what you're seeing is an electrical discharge that happens between two charge centers, one positive and the other negative. These two centers can be two clouds, or a cloud and the ground, or even just one cloud if all the positive particles are in one area of that cloud and all the negative ones are in another area of the same cloud.

When lightning bolts flash through the air they heat up the area they pass through. Thunder is the sound wave produced by the rapid expansion of air that's been suddenly heated up by the lightning bolt.

If clouds are filled with water, how can they float?

Clouds are made up of tiny water droplets so small that they can only be seen with a microscope. These minidrops don't weigh much, so they—and therefore a cloud of them—can be kept aloft by warm air rising from the earth. But when many of these droplets cling together, forming a large drop of water, they're too heavy to stay up. When that happens, it's time to get out your umbrella.

Where does dew come from?

You can make your own dew just by taking a cold pitcher of water out of the refrigerator on a hot day. Tiny beads of water, like the beads you see on grass on summer mornings, form on the outside of the pitcher. When warm, moist air touches the cold pitcher—or the cold grass—the air cools down too. Cool air can't hold as much moisture as warm air, so some of the water drops out onto the cold surface.

Index

Picture Credits

pp. 4-5 Stouffer Enterprises/ Animals, Animals (cedar waxwings) 6-7 Tony Thomas. 8-9 Lynda Cooper. 10-11 Elaine Macpherson; Lynda Cooper; Mary Carrick; Olena Kassian. 12-13 S. C. Bisserot/ Bruce Coleman Inc. 14-15, 16-17 Joe Weissmann. 18-19 Tony Thomas. 20-21 Joe Weissmann. 22-23 Clive Dobson/Fifty Fingers Inc. 24-25 NASA. 26-27 Fred Uni/Animals Animals (screech owl); Patti Murray/Animals Animals (anhinga). 28-29 Michael C. T. Smith/Photo Researchers Inc. (emperor penguin). 30-31 Stouffer Enterprises/Animals Animals (cedar waxwings); Townsend P. Dickinson/Photo Researchers. Inc. (Arctic tern); Ted Levin/ Animals Animals (Atlantic puffin) 32-33 Kim LaFavre; Olena Kassian. 34-35 Dwight Kuhn. 36-37 Julian Mulock. 38-39 Olena Kassian. 40-41 Olena Kassian; Elaine Macpherson; Anker Odum. 42-43 John Foster.

Front Cover: J.L. Lepore/ Photo Researchers, Inc. (Common Puffin)
Back Cover: Michael & Barbara Reed/Animals Animals

Consultants

Roy Anderson, Department of Zoology, University of Guelph; Allan Baker, Department of Ornithology, Royal Ontario Museum; Peter Beamish, Ceta-Research; Ron Brooks, Department of Zoology, University of Guelph; Centre for UFO Studies, Evanston, Illinois; Jim Dick, Department of Ornithology, Royal Ontario Museum; Terry Dickinson; John Grayson, Department of Physiology, Faculty of Medicine, University of Toronto; Peter Hallett, Department of Physiology, Faculty of Medicine, University of Toronto; Herzberg Institute of Astrophysics, Ottawa, Ontario; Bruce Hunter, Department of Clinical Studies, University of Guelph; Ross James, Department of Ornithology, Royal Ontario Museum; Finn Larsen, Vancouver Public Aquarium;, Ross MacCulloch, Department of Ichthyology and Herpetology, Royal Ontario Museum; Brian Marshall, Department of Entomology, Royal Ontario Museum; Susan McIver, Department of Zoology, University of Toronto; D. H. Osmond, Department of Physiology, Faculty of Medicine, University of Toronto; John Parker, Toronto General Hospital; Robert Schemenauer, Environment Canada; Morris Smith, Department of Environmental Biology, University of Guelph; Ian Stirling, Canadian Wildlife Service; R. W. Stonehouse, the cat doctor; Michael Thompson, Department of Chemistry, University of Toronto; Elizabeth Wilson, Department of Clinical Studies, University of Guelph; Patrick Woo, Department of Zoology, University of Guelph.

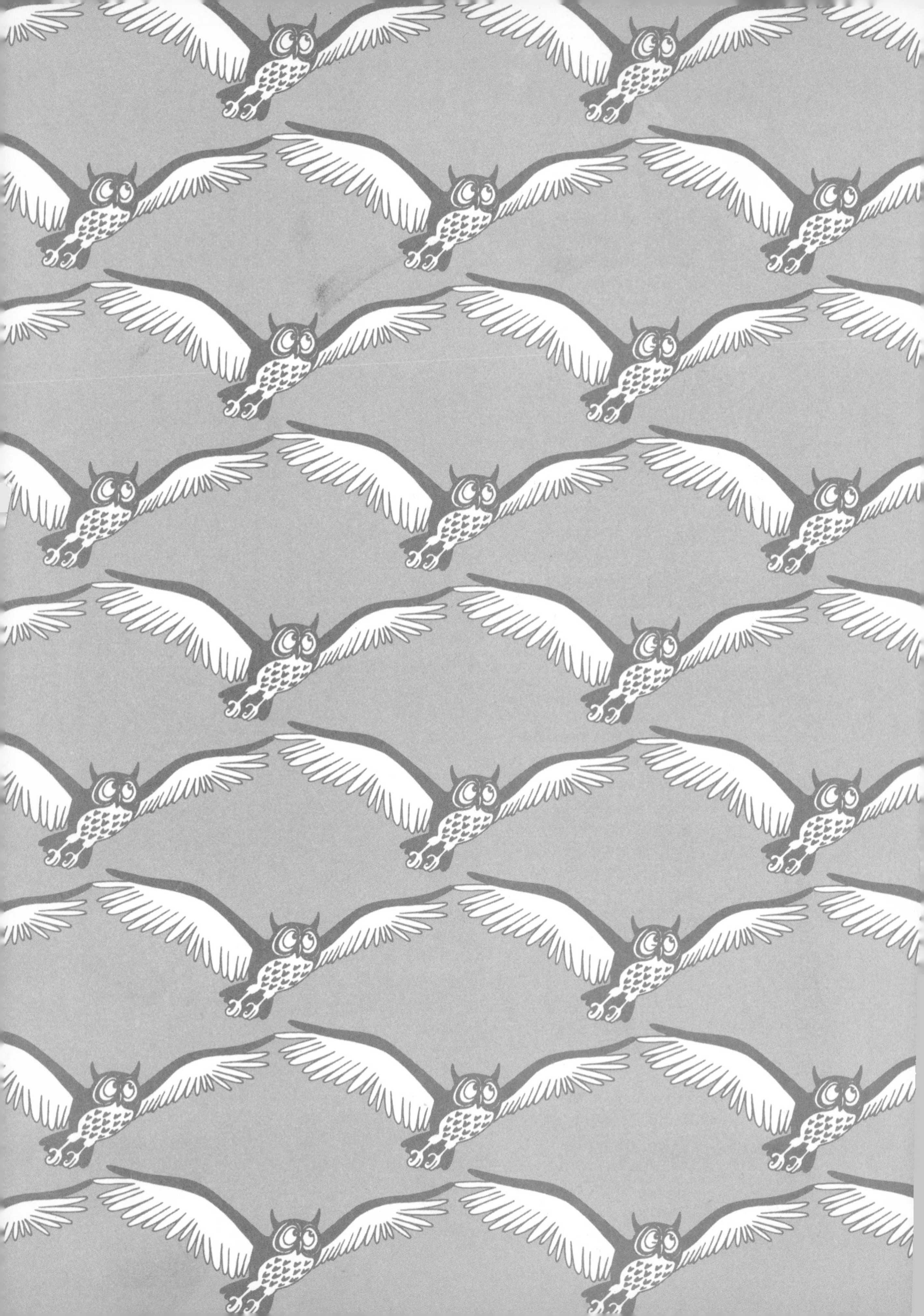